Kingdom
of GOD

FRENCH STROTHER

KINGDOM OF GOD

iUniverse books may be ordered through booksellers or by contacting:

iUniverse
1663 Liberty Drive
Bloomington, IN 47403
www.iuniverse.com
844-349-9409

ISBN: 978-1-6632-0987-0 (sc)
ISBN: 978-1-6632-0986-3 (e)

Library of Congress Control Number: 2020918703

Print information available on the last page.

iUniverse rev. date: 10/21/2020

Contents

Introduction

I am not a pastor, leader in a church, theologian, or commentary for scripture. I am a Christian baptized with the Holy Spirit that was given a task by God to do. The commission came to me through several visions but mostly by the Holy Spirit.

I am going to try to explain my task by using this analogy. There is a train with 2.4 billion Christian on it. Satan derailed the train with one verse in the Bible. The Christian will not get to the end of times unless the train is put back on its track. By getting the train on its way, the Christians will see the truth and can grow. Somehow Satan blinded the eyes and closed the ears of the Christians when they read that verse. God called on me without a crew to put the train back on the track. God told me to go among the Christians on the train, and I will find those that will realize the Truth and help me. God said that the task would be massive, but I will find leaders or want to be leaders to assist me.

The one verse that Satan used to derail the Church is when Jesus was talking to Nicodemus. The verse is John 3:5 it states: "Jesus answered, "Most assuredly, I say to you unless one is born of water and the Spirit, he cannot enter the kingdom of God." That verse is telling how Christians can be born-again. It is not saying that those who are saved are born-again. There is nowhere in the Bible that says a person being just saved is born-again. You have pastors and leaders put a spin on it to make you think it is. God's words are amazingly simple and straightforward; there is no need to spin it. Some pastors and leaders are becoming like politicians turning the subject to mean what they want.

Those that are saved become a new creation/creature. 2 Corinthians 5:17 states: "Therefore, if anyone *is* in Christ, *he is* a new creation; old things have passed away; behold, all things have become new." How can a person be born-again when they are a new creation/creature? Was humanity born-again when God created man? Humanity is born-again every time a baby is born. Just the word new in the new creation is letting you know that you are the first of its kind. If you are the first of its kind, how can you be born-again? I will give more information in the book.

My book is about the Kingdom of God. I have to give you some essential information, but there is a lot more to know. What is the difference between the Kingdom of God and the Kingdom of Heaven? What is the difference between the Gospel of Christ and the Gospel of God? What is the purpose of the Kingdom of Priests in the Old Testament? Who are the ones that are going to be kings and priests? Who are the two witnesses in the book of Revelation? You will have the answers to these questions and more. Of course, your answers now are different because you did not have the Truth to the verse John 3:5.

You do not have to be a pastor, educator, or someone with long credentials to understand God's Word. If the Holy Spirit has baptized you, the Spirit of Truth will reveal God's Word to you. Salvation is not the baptism with the Holy Spirit. Many that are baptized with the Holy Spirit are missing the Truth when they hear it. I have researched some great leaders in the Church that are baptized with the Holy Spirit that is so close in getting a complete Truth. I believe that when they read my book or even this introduction, the Truth will be absolute in them.

My book starts with several chapters by giving you information about man's spirit and the physical man. Then I will provide you with different things that are connected to the Kingdom of God.

Fully God and Fully man

There are many people, including leaders of church organizations that do not understand how Jesus can be fully God and fully man at the same time. An excellent place to start to understand was in the book of Genesis when the man was created.

Genesis 2:6 states:

> "And the LORD God formed man of the dust of the ground and breathed into his nostrils the breath of life, and man became a living being."

The physical man is formed from the dust of the ground, and the spirit man came when the Lord God breathed into his nostrils the breath of life. From the beginning, you could say that man is part of heaven and part earth. John 4:24 states that "God is Spirit." So, if God is a Spirit, then Jesus is a Spirit, which means He is entirely God as a Spirit. Now the man was created with two parts, spirit man and physical man. Jesus is God in the flesh. The flesh is physical man that came from His mother, Mary.

Jesus's mother, Mary, was told by an angel that she was highly favored and blessed among women. The angel said to her that she would conceive in her womb and bring forth a Son. His name shall be called Jesus. Mary told the angel that she had not known a man. Then Luke 1:35 states:

> "And the angel answered and said to her, "The Holy
> Spirit will come upon you, and the power of the Highest
> will overshadow you; therefore, also, that Holy One who
> is to be born will be called the Son of God."

I believe that the best way to see Jesus as God and man is in 1 John 5:6. It states:

> "This is He who came by water and blood—Jesus Christ;
> not only by water but by water and blood. And it is the
> Spirit who bears witness because the Spirit is Truth."

The above verse shows that water represents God, and blood represents man. It is interesting because it tells us that the only common thing in man is the blood. Also, it is telling us that each person's spirit is different. It is clear to me that Jesus is fully God and full man.

Some might ask, how can God be in a baby? That is an excellent question. In the Bible, there is a reference that Jesus grew in stature. I believe that Jesus's Spirit, along with His physical body, increased in size. I was around twelve years old when I saw my first vision, and it was of a young boy. I believe that man's spirit grows to be approximately twenty years old, but the physical man continues to age.

Luke 2:52 states:

> "And Jesus increased in wisdom and stature, and in favor
> with God and men."

From the beginning of man's creation, the physical man was subjected to aging and not the spiritual man. I believe that the spirit man will not get older than the age when Adam was created. God made man live forever, but because of disobedience, the man was punished. God tells us that man's physical body will die.

Genesis 3:19 states:

> "In the sweat of your face, you shall eat bread till you return to the ground, For out of it you were taken; for dust you are, and to dust, you shall return."

Contrary to what some may say, this physical body of flesh and blood will not be going to Heaven.

1 Corinthians 15:50 states:

> "Now this I say, brethren, that flesh and blood cannot inherit the kingdom of God; nor does corruption inherit incorruption."

There is nowhere in the book of Genesis states that the spirit man will die. But there is a separation from God. God's concerns about the tree of life were for the physical man because the spirit man will live forever in the garden or out of the garden. In other words, the spirit man will live forever in Heaven or hell.

There is nowhere in the Bible that I know of that gives Adam and Eve ages at creation. I believe indirectly, the ages of Adam and Eve are given. Also, the age of Jesus's mother Mary is not shown when she conceived Him. But based on the tradition during that time, Mary would have been around the age of sixteen years old. God told Adam and Eve to be fruitful and multiply. Then it is evident that Eve was of childbearing age, around the age of sixteen of age at the time of creation. The age of sixteen sounded reasonable for the physical man but not for the spirit man. For example, a young man at sixteen can make a young woman pregnant. But he was five feet ten inches tall and grew to six feet two inches between the ages of eighteen and twenty-one years old. Also, I just want to say a girl reaches maximum growth height faster than a boy. Of course, I will use the range between eighteen and twenty-one of age to determine Adam's age. Eve was created from Adam's rib. The reason that I used the concept of maximum height growth because the spirit part of Adam did not grow anymore when placed into the physical part. You could not put a five-foot spirit man in a six-foot physical man's body and say that it is perfect. I do not believe that the age when Jesus's mother, Mary's conception with Him, would be different from the age in Adam and Eve's creation. Here is an incident that God allowed me to see that could help in what I am trying to say. I called it Forever Young.

Forever Young

It started as a typical day. I was sitting in my recliner in the bedroom, reading over some papers, and watching television. My wife was downstairs watching her tv shows in the family room. It was late morning on a November 2019 sunny day with the curtains and blinds open.

I heard my wife walking down the hallway toward the master bedroom. I looked up and watched her as she entered the room. As she entered the room, I noticed a transparent figure walking in the back of her but a little to the side. My wife continued to walk past me about five feet away. The figure came toward me and stood inches from my right leg. I looked at the figure as it approached me, but it seems not to look down at me. It stood there for about ten or more seconds staring out the window.

Yes, the figure was transparent, but it appeared to be wearing pastel color clothes. The surprisingly impressive appearance about the figure looked like my wife when she was about twenty years old. My wife is in her sixties now. The figure vanished, and I turned immediately and looked at my wife. My reaction was based on an event that took place about two weeks before this vision.

There was a frightening incident that happened about two weeks before the vision. My wife awoke me when she jumped up when she could not breathe. I immediately went to her, and she was holding her chest and pointing to her throat. I did not grasp what was going on at first because she could not talk. She started to walk to the bathroom, then to the closet and back to the bedroom. She looked at me and gave me a big hug while she still could not breathe. I started to hit her on her back rapidly, and she began to get some oxygen in her lungs. Then she could sit down to relax and calm down. She adamantly refused to go to the hospital or the doctor in the morning.

You could say that I was in a red alert mode up to and several weeks after the vision. I was continually checking to make sure she was alright. I was sleeping less at night. The least little movement of her changing positions in bed would awake me. Even when she coughed, I would wake up. I am so happy that we already had a monitor in the family room to check on the dogs from the master bedroom. So, if there were a sporting event, I could still watch her through the monitor. I began to spend more time looking at her shows to be there if she had an episode. If I did not see her from the monitor, I immediately would go downstairs or yelled to see where she was. It was frustrating to her, always asking is she okay.

Now you have a better understanding of my mindset when I saw this vision. When the figure vanished, I immediately looked around for my wife. At this moment, I did not know if she was still alive or passed and gone to Heaven. Filled with emotion, I turned and saw that she was standing by the bed. I was emotional internally but trying to be calm externally. We spoke for a few minutes, and then she got what she needed. As she left to go downstairs, I just stared at her until I could not see her on the steps. At that moment, tears ran down my face while I watched her through the monitor. I washed my face and calmed myself. Then I went downstairs and watched my wife's shows with her.

Let me say, and this is not the first time I have seen a spiritual vision. I saw my first spirit vision when I was about twelve years old. I wrote a book on my visions up to the year 2015. The vision in 2012 and this vision in the winter of 2019 are at the top of being the most exciting. Mainly because they walked toward me, and I could've touched them, but I chose not to.

I have heard of the spirit leaving your body while you were sleeping but not awake. From reading the Bible, I know that the spirit leaves your body when you die. That is the reason why I was so emotional about my wife's spirit. I thought she was going to die at that moment. Now I do not want to give you scriptures to justify anything; all I want is to tell my story.

I prayed and asked the Lord why I saw this vision. It was always on my heart because I never heard anyone speak about your spirit walking alongside you. My wife has not had another incident of being able not to breathe. And she was getting more frustrated each day about me asking if she was okay.

I believe that the Lord answered my concerns about the vision. As with many of us, we missed the reason the first time from the Lord. Not because it is so complicated but because it is given to us straightforward. Many of us believe that God's answers are detailed, and only the Theologians, Priest, and Ministers are the only ones capable of understanding it. But God's solutions are simple, and you must put yourself in the mindset to receive it. During my daily routine of watching sermons on the television, my question was answered. The minister was speaking about our spirits in Heaven are young. Even if you die at the age of ninety-five, your spirit will be youthful in Heaven. His statement went entirely over my head with the connection of my vision. I saw this sermon about three weeks after my vision. My mindset was not in a receiving mode.

Most likely, the Lord had given me the answer several times, but I was not receiving it. So, the Lord allowed me to receive a vision like the previous one. And this time I was sitting in my wife's recliner in the family room. The family room has a cathedral ceiling so you can see the walkway coming from the stairs. My wife came out of one of the guest bedrooms and walked toward the master bedroom. As she came out of the bedroom, the same spirit figure that I saw previously was behind her like before. But this time, I did not see the pastel colors. About halfway down the hall toward the master bedroom, the spirit turned toward the family room balcony. It did not look down at me, but it seemed to look toward the window. As my wife entered the master bedroom, the figure vanished.

Several days later, I believe that I finally put the pieces together to answer my question. Why did I see my wife's spirit? Before the first vision of my wife's spirit, we were in the family room talking about the pictures on the wall. We talked about how much we aged and gain weight over the years. For me, my hair is white, and I gained fifty plus pounds since we were married. We laughed, joked, and reminisce about past events. I connected the sermon that our spirits are young in Heaven. After seeing the visions, you can say our spirits are young here on earth, even though we look old physically.

Yes, our spirits are perfection in comparison to our physical bodies. As I stated before, my wife is in her sixties, and she has difficulty walking. My wife's spirit was young, walked with good posture, and appeared in good physical shape. So, all of us that have some type of physical handicap now know that our spirit is a perfect physical specimen.

Seeing in the Spirit World

Yes, God blessed and allowed me to see spirit beings. I have been seeing spirit beings since around the age of twelve years old. Maybe I should say God allows me to see into the spirit world because I have seen other spiritual things. My first vision was of a little boy. Well, I guess you could say that a spirit being grows to be a certain age but never old. I have seen spirit beings at various height throughout my life but never old. So, I do not know how to explain to others seeing an older relative in Heaven. I believe that everyone should get pictures of their parents and grandparents when they were young adults to recognize them when you get to Heaven. I believe that anyone that died as a young child their spirit will continue to grow into a young adult. If Adam and Eve were placed in the garden as a young adult and never age, why do you expect your spirit to grow old?

Here is a mystery that many pondered over why no one recognized Jesus after His resurrection? Yes, he had a glorified body, but His glorified body was placed over His young Spirit body around twenty-one. That is the reason why Jesus still had the wounds on Him from the crucifixion so that they could recognize Him. Also, they could recognize Him after He spoke to them.

Shadows and Types

There are a lot of shadows and types in the Old Testament that coincide within the New Testament. Moses tabernacle is an especially important type that needs to be applied in the New Testament. God wanted the whole nation of Israel to become priests. God gave Moses a message on Mount Sinai to give to the children of Israel. Exodus 19:5,6 state:

> *"Now, therefore, if you will indeed obey My voice and keep My covenant, then you shall be a special treasure to Me above all people; for all the earth is Mine.* ⁶ *And you shall be to Me a **kingdom of priests** and a holy nation.' These are the words which you shall speak to the children of Israel."*

A kingdom of priests was so important to God that He called it a special treasure to Him. When they have become priests, they could go to other nations to spread God's word. But because of their sinful ways, it never happened as He would like. The nation of Israel did not come close to become priests. But God still wanted His people to become priests in the New Testament dispensation. So, we must closely follow all the steps because they will be applied in the New Testament dispensation. Just remember that we are looking at a type. The Tabernacle of Moses is a physical type that will be the **spirit** in the New Testament dispensation. Every aspect of the priest's way of life in the Old Testament is physical, but it changes to spirit way of life in the New Testament down to walking in the spirit.

Moses ordained Aaron and his sons along with consecrating the things inside the tabernacle. Moses conducted a sin offering, washed Aaron, and his sons with water, and anointed each one with oil. Also, he anointed all the things inside the tabernacle with oil. These three steps performed on Aaron and his sons to become priests are extraordinarily necessary. Without these three steps, they would not be permitted to enter the tabernacle. Aaron's sons could enter the first part of the tabernacle, but only Aaron, the high priest, could enter the second part of the tabernacle. Exodus 26:33 states:

> "And you shall hang the veil from the clasps. Then you shall bring the ark of the Testimony in there, behind the veil. The veil shall be a divider for you between the holy place and the Most Holy."

Being holy had to do with all aspects of your life. It had to do with what was clean and unclean or pure and impure. Even there were designated foods that were cleaned and uncleaned. If an Israelite ate uncleaned food, they had to wash with water and stay away from the campsite for a period. Also cleaned and uncleaned dwelt with anything you touched. Like something dead, bodily fluids, or anything involving death makes you impure. The Israelites had to wash with water and stay away from the campsite for a length of time. Being uncleaned or impure for a priest was unthinkable because he was always close to the tabernacle or inside the tabernacle. There standard of living was paramount to be in the presence of God. Also, moral standards were extremely high. The priests had to conduct every ritual without deviation from God's commands. Two of Aaron's sons deviated from God's command, and they were destroyed on the spot. You just read the physical type the way of life of the priest. Christians' way of life as a priest would be walking in the spirit.

Three Baptisms

I want to focus on the three steps that the priests must go through to enter the tabernacle. The three steps are performing a sin offering, washing with water, and the anointing of oil. Just remember these are physical types of what will occur in the New Testament but in the spirit. These steps represent the three baptisms in the New Testament. If these steps were so essential to becoming a priest in the Old Testament, why do so many fail to complete all three steps in the New Testament dispensation? The sin offering is a type of salvation today. The Holy Spirit baptizes you into Jesus Christ. There are many people today that have a problem in explaining salvation. Instead of saying that they are Christian and what makes them Christian, they would state their denomination. Denomination of a church has nothing to do in making you a Christian. The second type of washing with water is water baptism today. It is mind-boggling that church organizations get this wrong. They know that John the Baptist baptized Jesus by submerging Him in water. So, why do they sprinkle water on the person's head and then call it water baptism? The third type, the anointing of oil, represents Jesus baptizing you in the Holy Spirit. The majority of church organizations confused this as being the same as the first type. In the New Testament dispensation, it is noticeably clear to me that salvation is the Holy Spirit baptizes you into Jesus. The Holy Spirit is doing the baptizing. The third step in the New Testament dispensation Jesus baptize you in the Holy Spirit. It is noticeable clear that Jesus is doing the baptizing. Here are some verses stating Jesus baptize you in the Holy Spirit.

Mark 1:8 states:

> *"I indeed baptized you with water, but He will baptize you with the Holy Spirit."*

John 1:33 states:

> *"I did not know Him, but He who sent me to baptize with water said to me, 'Upon whom you see the Spirit descending, and remaining on Him, this is He who baptizes with the Holy Spirit."*

Matthew 3:11 states:

> *"I indeed baptize you with water unto repentance, but He who is coming after me is mightier than I, whose sandals I am not worthy to carry. He will baptize you with the Holy Spirit and fire."*

Luke 3:16 states:

> *"John answered, saying to all, "I indeed baptize you with water; but One mightier than I is coming, whose sandal strap I am not worthy to loose. He will baptize you with the Holy Spirit and fire."*

Acts 1:5 states:

> *"for John truly baptized with water, but you shall be baptized with the Holy Spirit not many days from now."*

The third step in the New Testament dispensation was so important that the four gospel books and the book of acts talked about it. A total of five times in five different books it was mentioned. We are supposed to be like Jesus, and He was baptized with the Holy Spirit.

Mark 1:10 states:

> "And immediately, coming up from the water, He saw the heavens parting and the Spirit descending upon Him like a dove."

John 1:32 states:

> "And John bore witness, saying, I saw the Spirit descending from heaven like a dove, and He remained upon Him."

Matthew 3:16 states:

> "When He had been baptized, Jesus came up immediately from the water; and behold, the heavens were opened to Him, and He saw the Spirit of God descending like a dove and alighting upon Him."

Luke 3:22 states:

> "And the Holy Spirit descended in bodily form like a dove upon Him, and a voice came from heaven which said, "You are My beloved Son; in You, I am well pleased."

The old and young people talked about the Holy Spirit descending like a dove on Jesus. There are movies with the Holy

Spirit descending on Jesus like a dove. I saw a movie where the minister had a boy in the Church's attic dropped down a live dove when he said the word Holy Spirit. Many know of the Holy Spirit, but only a few are being taught the Holy Spirit's characteristics.

Born Again

I guess that the best place to start about the Holy Spirit is when Jesus teaches Nicodemus.

John 3:1-7 state:

> "There was a man of the Pharisees named Nicodemus, a ruler of the Jews. ² This man came to Jesus by night and said to Him, "Rabbi, we know that You are a teacher come from God; for no one can do these signs that You do unless God is with him."

> ³ Jesus answered and said to him, "Most assuredly, I say to you, unless one is born again, he cannot see the kingdom of God."

> ⁴ Nicodemus said to Him, "How can a man be born when he is old? Can he enter a second time into his mother's womb and be born?"

> ⁵ Jesus answered, "Most assuredly, I say to you unless one is born of water and the Spirit, he cannot enter the Kingdom of God. ⁶ That which is born of the flesh is flesh, and that which is born of the Spirit is spirit. ⁷ Do not marvel that I said to you, 'You must be born again."

That was an extraordinary statement made by Jesus – unless one is born again, he cannot see the Kingdom of God. But this next statement is where the problem starts with the majority of church organizations. Jesus said unless one is born of water and of the Spirit, he cannot enter the Kingdom of God. Jesus knew that He had to make the second statement about being born of water and the Spirit. So many people believe that just believing in Jesus, you will enter the Kingdom of God. The part about being born of water cannot be water baptism because He said what is born of the Spirit is spirit. Water baptism is not a spirit. Jesus is talking about the first and third baptisms. He is talking about the Holy Spirit baptizing you into Jesus, which is salvation, and Jesus baptizing you in Holy Spirit, which is the filling of the Holy Spirit.

1 John 5:6 states:

> *"This is He who came by water and blood—Jesus Christ;*
> *not only by water, but by water and blood. And it is the*
> *Spirit who bears witness, because the Spirit is Truth."*

In the above scripture, Jesus came by water and blood. The water was the spirit part of Him, and blood was the physical part of Him. Jesus used water to represent Himself. Jesus has two commonalities in Him. One is the blood, which is a commonality to mankind coming from Mary, His mother. Two is the water, which is a commonality to God coming through the Holy Spirit. You cannot be born-again unless you have a commonality to something. Luke 1:35 states:

> *"And the angel answered and said to her, "The Holy*
> *Spirit will come upon you, and the power of the Highest*
> *will overshadow you; therefore, also, that Holy One who*
> *is to be born will be called the Son of God."*

17

This is exciting because those that are in Christ is a new creation. 2 Corinthians 5:17 states:

> *"Therefore, if anyone is in Christ, he is a new creation; old things have passed away; behold, all things have become new."*

Now we know that the commonality between Christ and the new creation (anyone is in Christ) must be water. Of course, you know when they say new creation is talking about Christians. It cannot be blood as the commonality because Jesus resurrected body did not have blood. And when we are taking up in Heaven, we will not have blood.

1 Corinthians 15:49,50 state:

> *"And as we have borne the image of the man of dust, we shall also bear the image of the heavenly Man. [50] Now this I say, brethren, that flesh and blood cannot inherit the kingdom of God; nor does corruption inherit incorruption."*

When Jesus said born of water and the Spirit, He was talking a Christian being baptized with the Holy Spirit. The commonality between the Christian and the Holy Spirit is water.

Jesus, speaking to the woman of Samaria at the well, indicates that water represents salvation. Jesus asked the woman for a drink of water. She told Him that there was nothing to draw the water, and the well is deep.

John 4:13,14 state:

> *Jesus answered and said to her, "Whoever drinks of this water will thirst again, [14] but whoever drinks the water*

that I shall give him will never thirst. But the water that
I shall give him will become in him a fountain of water
springing up into everlasting life."

Initially, Jesus said that with physical water, you would thirst again, but the spirit water He gives you will never thirst. His water will become in you, springing up into everlasting life. That is, without a doubt, talking about salvation.

John 3:16 states:

"For God so loved the world that He gave His only
begotten Son, that whoever believes in Him should not
perish but have everlasting life."

So, you could write the second statement to Nicodemus like this - unless one is born of Jesus and the Holy Spirit, you cannot enter the Kingdom of God. Now that would be more in line with the tabernacle of Moses. It is a hard truth for many church organizations because they do not recognize the baptism of the Holy Spirit. And those church organizations that acknowledge it do not understand the Truth.

Jesus said to the Samaritan woman for salvation is of the Jews, and then He said in John 4:23,24 -

"But the hour is coming, and now is, when the true
worshipers will worship the Father in spirit and Truth;
for the Father is seeking such to worship Him. 24 God is
Spirit, and those who worship Him must worship in spirit
and Truth."

Jesus is telling the Samaritan woman that there is more than salvation to be a true worshiper. Spirit and Truth are referring to the Holy Spirit. It is only a Christian that can receive the spirit and Truth from the Holy Spirit. The true worshiper is the one that is born of water and the Spirit.

John 14:16-17

> *"And I will pray the Father, and He will give you another Helper, that He may abide with you forever—* [17] *the Spirit of truth, whom the world cannot receive, because it neither sees Him nor knows Him; but you know Him, for He dwells with you and will be in you."*

I do not know how Satan did it, but the Church must have had a shield over their eyes and earplugs in their ears because they did not understand what Jesus was telling Nicodemus. I have read many commentaries, watched many sermons, and asked Christians to interpret the conversation between Jesus and Nicodemus. Everyone believes that being born-again is just salvation. They think that the New Testament books are about salvation. No, the New Testament is about Christians becoming priests. The Kingdom of God is the spiritual aspect of the Kingdom of priests in the Old Testament dispensation. God said that the Kingdom of priests is a special treasure to Him.

Even in the Lord's Prayer, it states that Father God is waiting for His Kingdom and the power. Matthew 6:9-13 state:

"Our Father in Heaven,
Hallowed be Your name.
[10] *Your Kingdom come.*
Your will be done
On earth as it is in Heaven.
[11] *Give us this day our daily bread.*
[12] *And forgive us our debts,*

As we forgive our debtors.
[13] *And do not lead us into temptation,*
But deliver us from the evil one.
For Yours is the Kingdom and the power and the glory forever. Amen."

The Promise

The promise was so significant that Jesus commanded the disciples not to leave Jerusalem. Throughout the Bible, when a promise was made, it was something special. Luke 24:49 states:

> "Behold, I send the Promise of My Father upon you; but tarry in the city of Jerusalem until you are endued with power from on high."

John 14:15-17 state:

> "If you love Me, keep My commandments. And I will pray the Father, and He will give you another Helper, that He may abide with you forever— the Spirit of Truth, whom the world cannot receive, because it neither sees Him nor knows Him; but you know Him, for He dwells with you and will be in you."

Acts 1:4 states:

> "And being assembled together with them, He commanded them not to depart from Jerusalem, but to wait for the Promise of the Father, "which," He said, "you have heard from Me."

Acts 2:33 states:

> "*Therefore, being exalted to the right hand of God, and having received from the Father the promise of the Holy Spirit, He poured out this which you now see and hear.*"

Ephesians 1:13 states:

> "*In Him you also trusted, after you heard the word of truth, the gospel of your salvation; in whom also, having believed, you were sealed with the Holy Spirit of promise.*"

The disciples returned to Jerusalem and had prayer in the upper room. There were one hundred and twenty in the room. Acts 2:1-4 state:

> "*When the Day of Pentecost had fully come, they were all with one accord in one place. ² And suddenly there came a sound from Heaven, as of a rushing mighty wind, and it filled the whole house where they were sitting. ³ Then there appeared to them divided tongues, as of fire, and one sat upon each of them. ⁴ And they were all filled with the Holy Spirit and began to speak with other tongues, as the Spirit gave them utterance.*"

They were speaking in other tongues so loudly that the people outside started to gather.

Acts 2:5-12 state:

> "*And there were dwelling in Jerusalem Jews, devout men, from every nation under Heaven. ⁶ And when this sound occurred, the multitude came together, and were confused, because everyone heard them speak in his own*

language. [7] *Then they were all amazed and marveled, saying to one another, "Look, are not all these who speak Galileans?* [8] *And how is it that we hear, each in our own language in which we were born?* [9] *Parthians and Medes and Elamites, those dwelling in Mesopotamia, Judea and Cappadocia, Pontus and Asia,* [10] *Phrygia and Pamphylia, Egypt and the parts of Libya adjoining Cyrene, visitors from Rome, both Jews and proselytes,* [11] *Cretans and Arabs—we hear them speaking in our own tongues the wonderful works of God."* [12] *So they were all amazed and perplexed, saying to one another, "Whatever could this mean?"*

Speaking in Tongue

I was attending a church service, and the pastor was criticizing Christians that spoke in tongues because no one could understand them. He claimed that they were speaking from Satan. Just because the people on the outside could hear their tongue being spoken at the disciple's time, he believed that is the way it should always be. The outsiders could understand in their tongue at the time of the disciples that a church environment was created. You must realize that the Church is the people and not the building. They all were hearing the wonderful works of God. In an organized church setting, if someone spoke in tongues, there was one or two that could interpret what was being said. If there were no interpreter, then the speaker would keep it to themselves. In 1 Corinthians, Paul spoke to an unorganized church explaining the proper procedure. It is evident that the pastor that I talked about experienced a disorganized church.

1 Corinthians 14;26 states:

> "How is it then, brethren? Whenever you come together, each of you has a psalm, has a teaching, has a tongue, has a revelation, has an interpretation. Let all things be done for edification."

1 Corinthians 14:27 states:

> "If anyone speaks in a tongue, let there be two or at the most three, each in turn, and let one interpret."

1 Corinthians 14:2 states:

> "For he who speaks in a tongue does not speak to men but to God, for no one understands him; however, in the spirit he speaks mysteries."

1 Corinthians 14:4-6 state:

> "He who speaks in a tongue edifies himself, but he who prophesies edifies the Church. I wish you all spoke with tongues, but even more that you prophesied; for he who prophesies is greater than he who speaks with tongues, unless indeed he interprets, that the Church may receive edification. But now, brethren, if I come to you speaking with tongues, what shall I profit you unless I speak to you either by Revelation, by knowledge, by prophesying, or by teaching?"

Another criticism by the pastor was the people that he saw speaking in tongues were out of control falling around. Contrary to what some may say, speaking in tongues is the only gift you control. Those that speak in tongues must learn how to manage their emotion when the spirit comes forth. It is the emotion of the physical body that is out of control, not the spirit. As stated by Apostle Paul, if there is no interpreter, pray in the spirit within yourself so that you do not interrupt the church service.

When I first started to speak in tongues, it sounded like gibberish to me. My first experience speaking in tongues was in my dorm at college. Yes, I had to get a grip on my emotion because

I did not want anyone to hear me. I was standing in the middle of the dorm room praising the Lord. I was already emotional before I started to speak in tongues. It took me by surprise, and my emotion elevated even more. At that time, I thought it was customary to get emotional because I saw it happened before. It took some time before my gibberish sounded like a language. I heard someone say this, think of your gibberish as a young child learning how to speak. The father of that child understands what that child is saying before anyone else can. He would interpret to his friends what the child is communicating with a smile on his face. Then I heard the person say, God, understands your gibberish from the first sound. The more you speak in tongues, the more apparent the words become. But you still will not know what you are saying unless you have the gift of interpretation. It was many years before I heard a minister explain that speaking in tongues is separate from your emotions. I believe from that point on. I started to speak in tongues often. Now I speak in tongues many hours each day without the emotion. I speak in tongues while watching the television, driving the car, and in the supermarket. It is an everyday thing for me now. I speak in tongues far more than I talk in English.

Spirit

In the spirit means it goes directly to God. Speaking in tongues is a language that you cannot learn. It is not a foreign language like you learn in school. No one can teach it to you. Speaking, singing, or worship in the spirit is easier than walking in the spirit. There is no battlefront within you when speak, sing, or worship in the spirit. But there will be battlefronts on the outside from those who do not know the Spirit of Truth. Now walking in the spirit, there is a significant confrontation with the flesh on the inside. And there are significant confrontations on the outside. You have all the sensory perceptions coming against you.

1 Corinthians 14:2 states:

> "For he who speaks in a tongue does not speak to men but to God, for no one understands him; however, in the spirit he speaks mysteries."

1 Corinthians 14:15 states:

> "What is the conclusion then? I will pray with the spirit, and I will also pray with the understanding. I will sing with the spirit, and I will also sing with the understanding."

Colossians 3:16 states:

> "*Let the word of Christ dwell in you richly in all wisdom, teaching and admonishing one another in psalms and hymns and spiritual songs, singing with grace in your hearts to the Lord.*"

Ephesians 5:19 states:

> "*speaking to one another in psalms and hymns and spiritual songs, singing and making melody in your heart to the Lord,*"

John 4:23 states:

> "*But the hour is coming, and now is, when the **true worshipers** will worship the Father in spirit and truth; for the Father is seeking such to worship Him.*"

John 4:24 states:

> "*God is Spirit, and those who worship Him must worship in spirit and truth.*"

Philippians 3:3 states:

> "*For we are the circumcision, who worship God in the Spirit, rejoice in Christ Jesus, and have no confidence in the flesh,*"

Galatians 5:16-21 state:

> "*I say then: Walk in the Spirit, and you shall not fulfill the lust of the flesh. For the flesh lusts against the Spirit,*

> *and the Spirit against the flesh; and these are contrary to one another, so that you do not do the things that you wish. But if you are led by the Spirit, you are not under the law. Now the works of the flesh are evident, which are: adultery, fornication, uncleanness, lewdness, idolatry, sorcery, hatred, contentions, jealousies, outbursts of wrath, selfish ambitions, dissensions, heresies, envy, murders, drunkenness, revelries, and the like; of which I tell you beforehand, just as I also told you in time past, that those who practice such things will not inherit the Kingdom of God."*

Many church organizations believe they were baptized in the Holy Spirit at the time of salvation. They would say that the Holy Spirit is in them because of Jesus Christ is in them. They have two different functions. Jesus Christ's Spirit is for salvation, and the Holy Spirit's function is to give you power. Jesus Himself did not have power until He received the baptism of the Holy Spirit. It is when the Holy Spirit descended on Him like a dove. After this, Jesus healed the sick and cast out demons. There is an outward evidence of seeing and hearing when you are filled with the Holy Spirit. In the New Testament dispensation, the outward evidence is speaking in tongues or prophecy.
Acts 19:6 states:

> *"And when Paul had laid hands on them, the Holy Spirit came upon them, and they spoke with tongues and prophesied."*

Acts 2:33 states:

> *"Therefore, being exalted to the right hand of God, and having received from the Father the promise of the Holy Spirit, He poured out this which you now see and hear."*

When the Holy Spirit came upon Jesus, there was an outward evidence of seeing and hearing. John the Baptist knew that Jesus was filled with the Holy Spirit because he saw and heard the outward evidence.

Luke 3:21,22 state:

> "When all the people were baptized, it came to pass that Jesus also was baptized; and while He prayed, the Heaven was opened. [22] And the Holy Spirit descended in bodily form like a dove upon Him, and a voice came from Heaven which said, "You are My beloved Son; in You I am well pleased."

Power

The primary function of the Holy Spirit is that He gives you power. Jesus told the disciples to stay in Jerusalem until they receive the power from the Holy Spirit.

Luke 24:49 states:

> *"Behold, I send the Promise of My Father upon you; but tarry in the city of Jerusalem until you are endued with power from on high."*

Acts 1:8 states:

> *"But you shall receive power when the Holy Spirit has come upon you; and you shall be witnesses to Me in Jerusalem, and in all Judea and Samaria, and to the end of the earth."*

1 Corinthians 4:20 states:

> *"For the **kingdom of God** is not in word but in power."*

Acts 10:38 states:

> *"how God anointed Jesus of Nazareth with the Holy Spirit and with power, who went about doing good and*

healing all who were oppressed by the devil, for God was with Him."

Acts 1:8 states:

"But you shall receive power when the Holy Spirit has come upon you; and you shall be witnesses to Me in Jerusalem, and in all Judea and Samaria, and to the end of the earth."

Romans 15:13 states:

"Now may the God of hope fill you with all joy and peace in believing, that you may abound in hope by the power of the Holy Spirit."

1 Thessalonians 1:5 states:

"For our gospel did not come to you in word only, but also in power, and in the Holy Spirit and in much assurance, as you know what kind of men we were among you for your sake."

Being like Christ

From an incredibly young age, I have heard ministers and pastors preached about being like Christ. I was timid but very observant of others around me. As I grew older, it became clear that the ministers, pastors, and congregations did not adhere to what was being preached repeatedly. Throughout the years, I noticed the ministers and pastors skipping over crucial points of the texts. They were taking things out of contexts to explain their views. Yes, their ideas would make the congregation clap their hands and yelled amen. I realized that many leaders were being performers and not preachers or teachers of the Word of God. The congregations did not know about what was happening because they did not read the word for themselves. The leaders would say a phrase occasionally that sounded like they knew the Word of God. They would use the words being like Christ or Christ-like many times. I am trying to say that millions and millions have listened to church organizations' leaders believing what they are saying is true without reading the Bible for themselves. Now we might be in this dilemma of not being told the truth for so long that many will be lost because people hate change. If we cannot get the Truth out, many Christians will not see or enter the Kingdom of God. I am deeply committed to telling the Truth that we all will be like Christ.

1 John 2:6 states:

> "*He who says he abides in Him ought himself also to walk just as He walked.*"

1 Peter 2:21 states:

> "*For to this you were called, because Christ also suffered for us, leaving us an example, that you should follow His steps:*"

1 Corinthians 11:1 states:

> "*Imitate me, just as I also imitate Christ.*"

Ephesians 5:1-2 state:

> "*Therefore, be imitators of God as dear children. And walk in love, as Christ also has loved us and given Himself for us, an offering, and a sacrifice to God for a sweet-smelling aroma.*"

Ephesians 4:22-24 state:

> "*that you put off, concerning your former conduct, the old man which grows corrupt according to the deceitful lusts, and be renewed in the spirit of your mind, and that you put on the new man which was created according to God, in true righteousness and holiness.*"

Romans 8:29 states:

> "*For whom He foreknew, He also predestined to be conformed to the image of His Son, that He might be the firstborn among many brethren.*"

Galatians 3:27 states:

> "For as many of you as were baptized into Christ have put on Christ."

1 John 3:2 states:

> "Beloved, now we are children of God; and it has not yet been revealed what we shall be, but we know that when He is revealed, we shall be like Him, for we shall see Him as He is."

2 Corinthians 3:18 states:

> "But we all, with unveiled face, beholding as in a mirror the glory of the Lord, are being transformed into the same image from glory to glory, just as by the Spirit of the Lord."

Galatians 2:20 states:

> "I have been crucified with Christ; it is no longer I who live, but Christ lives in me; and the life which I now live in the flesh I live by faith in the Son of God, who loved me and gave Himself for me."

1 John 4:17 states:

> "Love has been perfected among us in this: that we may have boldness in the day of judgment; because as He is, so are we in this world."

Luke 6:40 states:

> *"A disciple is not above his teacher, but everyone who is perfectly trained will be like his teacher."*

1 Peter 2:9 states:

> *"But you are a chosen generation, a royal priesthood, a holy nation, His own special people, that you may proclaim the praises of Him who called you out of darkness into His marvelous light."*

2 Corinthians 5:17 states:

> *"Therefore, if anyone is in Christ, he is a new creation; old things have passed away; behold, all things have become new."*

Kingdom of God

God's breakdown for His people is the same in the Old Testament and the New Testament. In the Old Testament, the Israelites are set apart from other nations. But the priests are set apart from the Israelites people. In the New Testament, Christians are set apart from the people of the world. But the priests (those Christians baptized with the Holy Spirit) are set apart from Christians. A different way to say it, born-again Christians are priests.

God made it clear in the Old Testament that He wanted a holy nation of priests that would be a special possession and treasure for Him. They would be set apart above all people for His purpose. He wanted to call the nation a Kingdom of Priests. He did not get His holy nation because the Israelites did not obey His voice and keep His covenant. The burnt offerings were not acceptable and pleasing to God.

Exodus 19:5-6 state:

> "Now, therefore, if you will indeed obey My voice and keep My covenant, then you shall be a special treasure to Me above all people; for all the earth is Mine. ⁶ And you shall be to Me a kingdom of priests and a holy nation.' These are the words which you shall speak to the children of Israel."

Exodus 19:5,6 state AMP state:

> *"Now, therefore, if you will in fact obey My voice and keep My covenant (agreement), then you shall be My own special possession and treasure from among all peoples [of the world], for all the earth is Mine; ⁶ and you shall be to Me a kingdom of priests and a holy nation [set apart for My purpose].' These are the words that you shall speak to the Israelites."*

God received His Kingdom of Priests spiritually in the New Testament. The Kingdom of God is the Kingdom of Priests spiritually. Jesus dying on the cross for our sins was the perfect sacrifice. Christians are being built up (born-again) into a spiritual house for a holy priesthood. They are special people for God's own possession. They are the chosen generation/race and a royal priesthood. God called His special people in the Old Testament priests, but in the New Testament, He called His special people royal priesthood. His chosen people are kings and priests.

1 Peter 2:4,5 state:

> *"Coming to Him as to a living stone, rejected indeed by men, but chosen by God and precious, ⁵ you also, as living stones, are being built up a spiritual house, a holy priesthood, to offer up spiritual sacrifices acceptable to God through Jesus Christ."*

1 Peter 2:9,10 state:

> *"But you are a chosen generation, a royal priesthood, a holy nation, His own special people, that you may proclaim the praises of Him who called you out of darkness." into His marvelous light; ¹⁰ who once were*

> *not a people but are now the people of God, who had not obtained mercy but now have obtained mercy."*

Now, I am going to show 1 Peter 2 in the AMP version. I believe you will understand it better.

1 Peter 2:4,5 AMP state:

> *"Come to Him [the risen Lord] as to a living Stone which men rejected and threw away, but which is choice and precious in the sight of God. ⁵ You [believers], like living stones, are being built up into a spiritual house for a holy and dedicated priesthood, to offer spiritual sacrifices [that are] acceptable and pleasing to God through Jesus Christ."*

1 Peter 2:9,10 AMP state:

> *"But you are A CHOSEN RACE, A royal PRIESTHOOD, A CONSECRATED NATION, A [special] PEOPLE FOR God's OWN POSSESSION, so that you may proclaim the excellencies [the wonderful deeds and virtues and perfections] of Him who called you out of darkness into His marvelous light. ¹⁰ Once you were NOT A PEOPLE [at all], but now you are GOD'S PEOPLE; once you had NOT RECEIVED MERCY, but now you have RECEIVED MERCY."*

I know that billions of people have not heard the Truth about the Kingdom of God. If they did, church organizations would be teaching it. Previously, I told you what Jesus said to Nicodemus. If a person is not born-again of water and the Spirit, they will not see or enter the Kingdom of God. Of course, He (Jesus) says that if you are not born-again of Jesus (Himself) and with the Holy Spirit, you cannot see or enter the Kingdom of God. Without a doubt, that statement is going to bring a chill to church organizations around the world. Before anyone becomes hostile, I want you to pray and ask God to reveal it to you as you read the scriptures. Hopefully, you will understand that you cannot have the Kingdom of God without baptism with the Holy Spirit, and you cannot have the baptism with the Holy Spirit without the Kingdom of God. All those church organizations saying that speaking in tongues is just for the Old Testament dispensation need to rethink their position. Flesh and blood will not inherit the Kingdom of God. The Holy Spirit gave Jesus power so that He could heal the sick and cast out demons.

The Kingdom of God did not start with Jesus until He was baptized with the Holy Spirit.

Mark 1:10-14 state:

> *"And immediately, coming up from the water, He saw the heavens parting and the Spirit descending upon Him like a dove. [11] Then a voice came from Heaven, "You are My beloved Son, in whom I am well pleased." [12] Immediately the Spirit drove Him into the wilderness. [13] And He was there in the wilderness forty days, tempted by Satan, and was with the wild beasts; and the angels ministered to Him. [14] Now after John was put in prison, Jesus came to Galilee, preaching the gospel of the Kingdom of God,"*

Jesus preached and spoke in parables throughout His ministry. During the last supper, He stated in Luke 22:16,18:

> [16] *"for I say to you, I will no longer eat of it until it is fulfilled in the Kingdom of God."*

> [18] *"for I say to you, I will not drink of the fruit of the vine until the Kingdom of God comes."*

When Jesus died on the cross and gave up His spirit, the veil in the temple was torn from the top to the bottom.

Mark 15:37,38 state:

> "And Jesus cried out with a loud voice and breathed His last. *38 Then the veil of the temple was torn in two from top to bottom.*"

At that moment, there was no divider between the Holy place and the Most Holy. All priests have access to Father God in the spirit. They can pray, sing, and worship the Father directly without Jesus being the mediator in the spirit. The priests are those that meet the requirements to enter the Kingdom of God. They are born of water and the Spirit.

Although Jesus said that it is easier for a camel to go through the eye of a needle than a rich man to enter the Kingdom of God, a rich man was waiting for the coming of the Kingdom of God. Also, he received Jesus's body and prepared it for burial.

Matthew 27:57,58 state:

> "Now when evening had come, there came a rich man from Arimathea, named Joseph, who himself had also become a disciple of Jesus. *58 This man went to Pilate and asked for the body of Jesus. Then Pilate commanded the body to be given to him.*"

Mark 15:43 states:

> "Joseph of Arimathea, a prominent council member, who was himself waiting for the kingdom of God, coming and taking courage, went in to Pilate and asked for the body of Jesus."

After His resurrection, Jesus preached and spoke of the things about the Kingdom of God. I believe that the scriptures in Mark 16:15-18 make it noticeably clear what Jesus was telling Nicodemus about being born of water and the Spirit. In verse 15, it states to preach the gospel is talking about the Kingdom of God. The next verse is fantastic in explaining the requirement for the Kingdom of God. Jesus said that he who believes and is baptized would be saved. We know as Christians that water baptism is not a requirement to believe in Jesus. Jesus was talking about the requirement for the Kingdom of God. He who believes in Jesus, which is salvation and is baptized with the Holy Spirit, can enter the Kingdom of God. Verses 17 and 18 confirm it by stating the signs that will follow those who believe in the Kingdom of God. They will receive power to cast out demons and heal the sick. Also, verse 17 clarifies to all Christians that they will speak with **new tongues** when they meet the requirement to enter the Kingdom of God.

Mark 16:15-18 state:

> "And He said to them, "Go into all the world and preach the gospel to every creature. [16] He who believes and is baptized will be saved; but he who does not believe will be condemned. [17] And these signs will follow those who believe: In My name they will cast out demons; **they will speak with new tongues**; [18] they will take up serpents; and if they drink anything deadly, it will by no means hurt them; they will lay hands on the sick, and they will recover."

Doing the forty days after His resurrection, He spoke about the things about the Kingdom of God.

Acts 1:3,4 state:

> "*to whom He also presented Himself alive after His suffering by many infallible proofs, being seen by them during forty days and speaking of the things pertaining to the kingdom of God. ⁴ And being assembled together with them, He commanded them not to depart from Jerusalem, but to wait for the Promise of the Father, "which," He said, "you have heard from Me;"*

1 Corinthians 4:20 states:

> "*The Kingdom of God is not in word but in power.*"

1 Corinthians 15:50 states:

> "*Now this I say, brethren, that flesh and blood cannot inherit the kingdom of God; nor does corruption inherit incorruption.*"

Romans 14:17 states:

> "*for the Kingdom of God is not eating and drinking, but righteousness and peace and joy in the Holy Spirit.*"

The above scripture gives a good example what born of water and the Spirit is. Anyone that is born of righteousness and peace (salvation) and joy of the Holy Spirit (baptized with the Holy Spirit) can enter the Kingdom of God.

Matthew 12:28 states:

> "*But if I cast out demons by the Spirit of God, surely the Kingdom of God has come upon you.*"

Mark 4:11 states:

> *"And He said to them, "To you it has been given to know the mystery of the kingdom of God; but to those who are outside, all things come in parables,"*

Mark 4:26.27 states:

> *"And He said, "The kingdom of God is as if a man should scatter seed on the ground, ²⁷ and should sleep by night and rise by day, and the seed should sprout and grow, he himself does not know how."*

Mark 9:1 states:

> *"And He said to them, "Assuredly, I say to you that there are some standing here who will not taste death till they see the Kingdom of God present with power."*

Matthew 6:33 states:

> *"But seek first the Kingdom of God **and** His righteousness, and all these things shall be added to you."*

In the above verse, Matthew 6:33 says to seek first the Kingdom of God and His righteousness. Jesus is telling you that you need more than salvation to enter the Kingdom of God. I believe that Jesus is saying anyone who does not meet the requirement for the Kingdom of God at least has His righteousness, meaning salvation. Before anyone says that I am teaching or preaching another gospel as Apostle Paul stated in Galatians 1:7,8 -

> *"which is really no gospel at all. Evidently some people are throwing you into confusion and are trying to pervert*

> the gospel of Christ. *8 But even if we or an angel from*
> *Heaven should preach a gospel other than the one, we*
> *preached to you, let them be under God's curse!"*

As stated in 1 Corinthians 4:20 – "The Kingdom of God is not in word but in power." It is about power, not teaching, and preaching the gospel of Christ. It is about healing and casting out evil spirits. That is the power the Holy Spirit gives you when you are filled in Him. Many people might believe it is a different gospel because they did not understand what Jesus meant when He said born of water and the Spirit. Father God wanted His people to become kings and priests, and that was the requirement. Of course, God knew that many would not meet the requirement but was saved. The Gospel of Christ is for getting Christians. Christians are the ones born of water. Christians must be baptized with the Holy Spirit (born-again) to enter the Kingdom of God.

Throughout the New Testament books, they talked about the gospel of Christ and the gospel of God. They are not the same. The gospel of Christ is about salvation. The gospel of God is about power of healing and casting out demons and other evil spirits. You must be a Christian to receive the baptism of the Holy Spirit. The world cannot receive the Holy Spirit.

The power of the Holy Spirit is especially important during the end time. In the book of Revelation it talks about the two witnesses. Revelation 11:3 states:

> *"And I will give power to my two witnesses, and they*
> *will prophesy one thousand two hundred and sixty days,*
> *clothed in sackcloth."*

There are three primary thoughts on the identity of the two witnesses in Revelation. (1) Moses and Elijah, (2) Enoch and Elijah, and (3) two believers that God calls to be His witnesses in the end times. I believe that the two witnesses are two groups of people that could be called two churches.

Revelation 11:4 states:

> *"These are the two olive trees and the two lampstands standing before the God of the earth."*

We know that in the first chapter of Revelation lampstands are referred to as churches. Jesus was telling John to write down what he sees, and then John turned around.

Revelation 1:11,12 state:

> *"saying, "I am the Alpha and the Omega, the First and the Last," and, "What you see, write in a book and send it to the seven churches which are in Asia: to Ephesus, to Smyrna, to Pergamos, to Thyatira, to Sardis, to Philadelphia, and to Laodicea." 12 Then I turned to see the voice that spoke with me. And having turned I saw seven golden lampstands,"*

The two groups referred to as churches have met the requirements to see and enter the Kingdom of God. They are Christians that are filled with the Holy Spirit with power. There will be two groups that will be the greatest among them that can see and enter the Kingdom of God. We know that there are different levels of intensity on born-again Christians (priests) in the Kingdom of God. Jesus made it clear when He made the statement that the least in the Kingdom of God is greater than John the Baptist. I believe there are many levels of born-again Christians inside and Christians outside the Kingdom of God.

Satan has suppressed the Christians from understanding the power of the Holy Spirit. Satan concealed the information from the beginning with the understanding of being born-again and the Kingdom of God. Born again is the two baptisms that are needed to see and enter the Kingdom of God. With the Spirit of Truth, you can see God putting things together for the end time. We must put the Truth out there about the Kingdom of God so that the number of kings and priests will increase because the end time is near.

There is something directly or indirectly in every book of the New Testament about the Kingdom of God.

Spirit of Truth

The Spirit of Truth, baptizing in the Holy Spirit, and the Kingdom of God are interwoven together. You cannot have one without the others. If you think you will see and enter the Kingdom of God, you will have the Spirit of Truth and must be baptized in the Holy Spirit. Being baptized in the Holy Spirit is the first step to acquiring the others. You cannot get the guidance of Truth if you have not been baptized in the Holy Spirit. There is no guidance of Truth is the reason why we have so many denominations throughout the world. If we believed in the Gospel of Jesus Christ, there would be one union with no denominations. Many Christians are going to say what about Romans 10:9 talking about salvation. I will get to that scripture later.

John 14:17 states:

> "*the Spirit of truth, whom the world cannot receive, because it neither sees Him nor knows Him; but you know Him, for He dwells with you and will be in you.*"

I heard a minister say that Jesus is a gift for the world and the Holy Spirit is a gift for the Christian. The world cannot receive the Spirit of Truth/Holy Spirit.

Ephesians 1:13 states:

"*In Him you also trusted, after you heard the word of truth, the gospel of your*

> salvation; in whom also, having believed, you were sealed
> with the Holy Spirit of promise."

1 John 5:6-8 states:

> "This is He who came by water and blood—Jesus Christ,
> not only by water, but by water and blood. And it is the
> Spirit who bears witness because the Spirit is Truth. [7] For
> there are three that bear witness in Heaven: the Father,
> the Word, and the Holy Spirit; and these three are one. [8]
> And there are three that bear witness on earth: the Spirit,
> the water, and the blood; and these three agree as one."

John 15:26 states:

> "But when the Helper comes, whom I shall send to you
> from the Father, the Spirit of truth who proceeds from
> the Father, He will testify of Me."

John 16:13 states:

> "However, when He, the Spirit of truth, has come, He
> will guide you into all truth; for He will not speak on
> His own authority, but whatever He hears He will speak;
> and He will tell you things to come."

2 Thessalonians 2:13 states:

> "But we are bound to give thanks to God always for
> you, brethren beloved by the Lord, because God from the
> beginning chose you for salvation through sanctification
> by the Spirit and belief in the truth."

1 John 4:6 states:

> "We are of God. He who knows God hears us; he who is not of God does not hear us. By this we know the spirit of Truth and the spirit of error."

Salvation

Before I start to explain Roman 10:9, let me show the text. Roman 10:9 states:

> *"that if you confess with your mouth the Lord Jesus and believe in your heart that God has raised Him from the dead, you will be saved."*

Along with other Christians, I have quoted this scripture many times. The verse Romans 10:9 is within the context that Israel needs the Gospel. Also, within the context that Moses writes about the righteousness which is of the law. Then it speaks about the righteousness of faith in Christ. You must realize that during Moses's time, the Israelites presented offerings to be sacrificed by the priest for the forgiveness of sins. It was a type of expression for the New Testament dispensation. Based on Romans 10:9, in faith, you will have salvation, which is true. That was based on a comparison during the time of Moses. And I believe that you are still saved, but it does not mean that you will see or enter the Kingdom of God. Jesus set the criteria for seeing and entering the Kingdom of God when He was speaking to Nicodemus. Romans 10:9 is about the gospel of Christ which is about salvation. Gospel of God is about the power and Kingdom of God. When we read the New Testament, you must look at key words to determine what gospel you are referring to.

The standard that Jesus set is based on Christians becoming priests. Now you can be saved and not become a priest. Looking back at the Tabernacle of Moses doing the priests' ordination, there were three things that they had to do. The three things were a sin offering, wash with water, and be anointed with oil. Of course, they are types for the three baptisms that we have today. Many church organizations do not recognize all three. Jesus did not say water baptism was a requirement to see or enter the Kingdom of God because it is not spirit but physical. Jesus said that to see or enter the Kingdom of God, you must be born of water and the Spirit, which both are spirit. You must accomplish both, not one of them to see or enter the Kingdom of God. You must meet the requirement that Jesus set. Throughout the book of Acts, people were asked did you receive the Holy Spirit since you believed. In other words, where you baptized in the Holy Spirit since you believed. When the Gentiles first received the baptism of the Holy Spirit, they were not baptized with water until after they received the Holy Spirit.

Acts 10:22,44-48 state:

> "And they said, "Cornelius the centurion, a just man, one who fears God and has a good reputation among all the nation of the Jews, was divinely instructed by a holy angel to summon you to his house and to hear words from you. [44] While Peter was still speaking these words, the Holy Spirit fell upon all those who heard the word. [45] And those of the circumcision who believed were astonished, as many as came with Peter, because the gift of the Holy Spirit had been poured out on the Gentiles also. [46] For they heard them speak with tongues and magnify God. Then Peter answered, [47] "Can anyone forbid water, that these should not be baptized who have received the Holy Spirit just as we have?" [48] And he commanded them to

> *be baptized in the name of the Lord. Then they asked him to stay a few days."*

I have heard many sermons stating that we will be kings and priests, not stating the requirement but only salvation. We must step up to the plate and teach the Truth. The Kingdom of God is salvation **and** being filled with the Holy Spirit with power.

Kingdom of Heaven

The Kingdom of Heaven has to do with righteousness, not about being born-again. Righteousness is about salvation. Matthew 5:10 states:

> *"Blessed are those who are persecuted for righteousness' sake, For theirs is the kingdom of heaven."*

Matthew 5:20 states:

> *"For I say to you, that unless your righteousness exceeds the righteousness of the scribes and Pharisees, you will by no means enter the kingdom of heaven."*

There is the Kingdom of Heaven for those who cannot see or enter the Kingdom of God. Before Jesus started His ministry preaching the Kingdom of God, John the Baptist preached about the Kingdom of Heaven. There is a scripture with Jesus stating that no one born from women is greater than John the Baptist, but the least in the Kingdom of God is greater than John the Baptist. Luke 7:28 states:

> *"For I say to you, among those born of women there is not a greater prophet than John the Baptist; but he who is least in the kingdom of God is greater than he."*

In the above verse, there are different levels of born-again

Christians, even in the Kingdom of God. So that reinforced what I said about Romans 10:9. Just being at the level of salvation is not higher enough for you to see or enter the Kingdom of God, which means that there are more steps for you to climb to see or enter the Kingdom of God. You must get to the point to see it, and then you must go farther to enter the Kingdom of God. As I stated before, those that enter the Kingdom of God will become kings and priests. They met the requirement of being born-again of water and the Spirit. They will be kings and priests over those that enter the Kingdom of Heaven.

Matthew 6:33 states:

> *"But seek first the kingdom of God **and** His righteousness, and all these things shall be added to you."*

Christians being born-again

Christians that are only saved still can meet the requirement of being born-again.

Ephesians 1:13 states:

> "In Him you also trusted, after you heard the word of truth, the gospel of your salvation; in whom also, having believed, you were sealed with the Holy Spirit of promise,"

You must confront the Father in Heaven with a sincere heart stating that you want to receive the baptism of the Holy Spirit.

Luke 11:12-14 states:

> "Or if he asks for an egg, will he offer him a scorpion? ¹³ If you then, being evil, know how to give good gifts to your children, how much more will your heavenly Father give the Holy Spirit to those who ask Him."

I was just praising God with a sincere heart, and I received the baptism in the Holy Spirit. I was surprised when I started to speak in tongues. There is an outward sign when you have been filled in the Holy Spirit. Usually, the sign is speaking in tongues, but you could also prophesize as a sign. Even in the Old Testament dispensation, there were outward signs when the Holy Spirit came upon them, but it did not remain. You only must be filled once with the Holy Spirit. Different gifts will manifest themselves at different times.

Mark 16:17 states:

> "And these signs will follow those who believe: In My name they will cast out demons; they will **speak with new tongues**."

1 Corinthians 12:7-11 state:

> "But the manifestation of the Spirit is given to each one for the profit of all: for to one is given the word of wisdom through the Spirit, to another the word of knowledge through the same Spirit, to another faith by the same Spirit, to another gifts of healings by the same Spirit, to another the working of miracles, to another prophecy, to another discerning of spirits, to another different kinds of tongues, to another the interpretation of tongues. But one and the same Spirit works all these things, distributing to each one individually as He wills."

Christians being born-again is the same as believers being baptized by the Holy Spirit. They are the same. The good news is that you met the requirement to enter the Kingdom of God. You have become a priest and will be a king to rule over the Kingdom of Heaven. God bless you!

Printed in the United States
By Bookmasters